NOV - 3 2011

D1283618

Monkey Business

TAMARINS

Gillian Gosman

PowerKiDS press.

New York

Published in 2012 by The Rosen Publishing Group, Inc.
29 East 21st Street, New York, NY 10010

First Edition

Editor: Jennifer Way
Book Design: Kate Laczynski

Photo Credits: Cover, pp. 1, 5, 6, 8, 9, 11, 12, 15, 22 Shutterstock.com; p. 4 iStockphoto/Thinkstock; p. 7 Visuals Unlimited, Inc./Thomas Marent/Getty Images; p. 10 © Thierry Montford/Peter Arnold, Inc.; pp. 11, 14 Oli Scarff/Getty Images; p. 13 © Luiz C. Marigo/Peter Arnold, Inc.; pp. 16–17 © J. & C. Sohns/age fotostock; p. 18 Raul Arboleda/AFP/Getty Images; p. 19 Bodo Marks/AFP/Getty Images; p. 20 Frederick Florin/AFP/Getty Images; p. 21 Hemera/Thinkstock.

Library of Congress Cataloging-in-Publication Data

Gosman, Gillian.
 Tamarins / by Gillian Gosman. — 1st ed.
  p. cm. — (Monkey business)
 Includes index.
 ISBN 978-1-4488-5021-1 (library binding) — ISBN 978-1-4488-5175-1 (pbk.) —
 ISBN 978-1-4488-5176-8 (6-pack)
 1. Tamarins—Juvenile literature. I. Title.
 QL737.P925G67 2012
 599.8'4—dc22

                                        2011000909

Manufactured in the United States of America

CPSIA Compliance Information: Batch #WS11PK: For Further Information contact Rosen Publishing, New York, New York at 1-800-237-9932

Contents

MEET THE TAMARIN

The tamarin is an interesting little **primate**. It moves easily between the high branches of trees. It digs with powerful fingers. It makes faces. It barks, whistles, and sings. Each sound it makes has a special meaning! Its dark, round eyes look this way and that. Its down-turned mouth looks thoughtful.

FUN FACT

The cotton-top tamarin of Colombia, in South America, is endangered. There are only about 1,000 of these monkeys in the wild.

Most tamarins are about the size of a squirrel.

Many **species** of tamarins are **endangered**. People have been killing them and clearing the forests where they make their homes for many years. People are working to help the tamarins, too, though. First, let's get to know this special animal!

The red-handed tamarin is also called the golden-handed tamarin. The fur on its paws can range from reddish orange to yellow.

5

TYPES OF TAMARINS

The emperor tamarin, with its white mustache, is easy to identify. Both males and females have these long, white whiskers.

There are many species of tamarin monkey. The emperor tamarin has long, white whiskers. The cotton-top tamarin has a puff of white fur on the top of its head. Saddleback tamarins have patterns of brown fur on their backs.

They may look very different, but the many species of tamarins have some things in common. Tamarins are some of the smallest monkeys. Most tamarins living in the wild are about 1 foot (30 cm) tall and weigh less than 1 pound (454 g).

The fur on saddle-back tamarins is a mix of brown, black, and black-and-white spots.

NEW WORLD MONKEYS

Tamarins are **New World** monkeys. New World monkeys are known for being more **primitive**, or simpler, than their **Old World** relatives. New World monkeys have smaller brains than do their Old World relatives. They are smaller in size, too.

The tamarin is closely related to another kind of

Cotton-top tamarins live in a small part of northwest Colombia.

New World monkey called the marmoset. Together, tamarins and marmosets are the most primitive of primates. Neither animal has an **opposable** thumb or a **prehensile** tail for gripping objects, as do some other kinds of monkeys. Both animals have thick fur, strong fingers, and long tails, though.

Marmosets, like the common marmoset shown here, are part of the same scientific family as tamarins.

LIVING IN THE TREES

Tamarins live in the rain forests and dry forests of South America. The rain forests where they are found are wet and hot. The dry forests where they are found are cooler.

Tamarins are **arboreal**. This means they spend almost all of their time in the trees. They sleep, eat,

The red-handed tamarin lives in Brazil, Guyana, French Guiana, and Suriname.

and play in the branches. Some species of tamarins have rounded, clawlike nails instead of the flat nails of most primates, including people. Their sharp nails help these tamarins grip and balance on tree branches.

Emperor tamarins are found in the rain forests of northern Bolivia, eastern Peru, and western Brazil.

WHAT TAMARINS EAT

Tamarins are **omnivores**. This means that they eat all kinds of food. They climb around in the trees to find food. Tamarins eat fruit, insects, and the juicy insides of plants.

In the morning, the monkeys move slowly from branch to branch. They return to spots where they have found food before. They might look for food

In zoos, tamarins are fed a mix of fruits, vegetables, mealworms, and special biscuits to make sure they get the vitamins they need.

for an hour or so, then stop for a nap. Each nap is longer than the one before it until noon. Then they take a long rest. In the late afternoon, they return to their home base and find a tree in which to sleep.

Spending a hot day climbing in trees and looking for food is tiring! That is why tamarins stop to rest throughout the day.

A GREAT GROUP

These tamarins are taking turns grooming each other's fur. Grooming is one way that social animals bond with other members of their group.

Tamarins are social animals. This means they live and play with one another. In the wild, they spend most of their time in a group of anywhere from 2 to 10 monkeys.

A group of tamarins is a little like a family. A male and a female monkey lead the group. They **mate**, or make babies, for the group. The whole group cares for these baby monkeys. The lead male and female also make decisions for the group to keep the group safe. Tamarins must always be on the lookout for **predators**. Large birds, wildcats, and snakes hunt them.

The crested caracara, shown here, is a bird that hunts monkeys like tamarins.

A DAY IN THE LIFE

Tamarins are **diurnal**. This means they are active during the day, and they go to sleep when the Sun sets. Tamarins sleep with their group in old animal nests or in large flowering plants. They wake just after the Sun rises. The whole sleeping group begins the day together.

After they wake up, the tamarins leave their sleeping tree and begin to look for food. They dig under tree

Tamarins move from tree to tree during their daily search for food. Here, an emperor tamarin hangs by its feet on the upper branches of a tree.

bark and poke their claws into flowers in search of food. They run along tree branches, leap from tree to tree, and swing from branches.

MALES AND FEMALES

Male and female tamarins look very much like each other. Within each tamarin species, both males and females will have the same fur patterns and markings. Males and females of the same species are generally about the same size, too.

Here are an adult male and female cottontop tamarin and their month-old offspring. They all share the same markings and fur patterns despite being different ages and sexes.

Very young tamarins stay close to their parents and other adults in the group. As they get bigger, they start to move around in the trees on their own.

Tamarins are adults and ready to mate when they are between 18 months and two years old. Tamarins can mate year-round. Mating happens most often between September and March, though. This is when the weather is warmest in the tamarins' habitat. Baby tamarins grow inside their mothers for about four months before being born.

BABY TAMARINS

Tamarin mothers may give birth to one baby or to **fraternal twins**. Sadly, one of the twins often dies during its first few months. In fact, in some tamarin species, less than half of all babies live longer than a year. They may be killed by predators or die when the group cannot find enough food for every monkey.

This male pied tamarin is carrying its 10-day-old babies. The babies are fraternal twins.

The young are raised by both parents and often by the other members of the group. The father often plays an important part in raising the young. Many male tamarin monkeys carry their babies on their backs between meals.

FUN FACT

In the wild, tamarins can live to be 15 years old.

A tamarin group's territory is generally between 74 and 99 acres (30–40 ha). That is one reason baby tamarins explore this area while riding on an adult's back!

TROUBLE FOR TAMARINS

Many species of tamarins are endangered. This means there are few of these monkeys living in the wild. They will die out unless steps are taken to help them.

South American rain forests are being cut down for their wood and to make way for farming. This is called deforestation. Deforestation takes away habitat from tamarins and other animals.

There is one main reason tamarins are in trouble. Large areas of rain forest have been cut down. Tamarins cannot live without plenty of room to find food, raise their young, and stay safe from predators. There are groups working to set aside places in South America's rain forests in the hope of keeping that habitat's plants and animals, such as the tamarins, from dying out.

Glossary

arboreal (ahr-BOR-ee-ul) Having to do with trees.

diurnal (dy-UR-nul) Active during the daytime.

endangered (in-DAYN-jerd) In danger of no longer existing.

fraternal twins (fruh-TER-nul TWINZ) Two babies that are born at the same time to one mother but that come from two different eggs.

mate (MAYT) To come together to make babies.

New World (NOO WURLD) North America and South America.

Old World (OHLD WURLD) The part of the world that includes Asia, Africa, and Europe.

omnivores (OM-nih-vawrz) Animals that eat both plants and animals.

opposable (uh-POH-zuh-bel) Able to hold digits on a hand or foot together.

predators (PREH-duh-terz) Animals that kill other animals for food.

prehensile (pree-HEN-sul) Able to grab by wrapping around.

primate (PRY-mayt) The group of animals that are more advanced than others and includes monkeys, gorillas, and people.

primitive (PRIH-muh-tiv) Less advanced.

species (SPEE-sheez) One kind of living thing. All people are one species.

Index

Web Sites

Due to the changing nature of Internet links, PowerKids Press has developed an online list of Web sites related to the subject of this book. This site is updated regularly. Please use this link to access the list: www.powerkidslinks.com/monk/tamarin/